Contents

Exciting Mexico

Mexico is a country that is found just south of the United States. Mexico is exciting and colourful. It has high mountains and pretty, sandy beaches. Mexico has an amazingly dramatic landscape that includes hot deserts, tropical forests and even active volcanoes.

The people of this dramatic country love to cook exciting food. Mexican food as we know it today started with the Mayans, one of the first groups of people to live in Mexico. The Mayans invented corn tortillas, which they ate with bean paste. Next came the Aztecs, who added chillies, honey, salt and cocoa to the Mexican diet.

When the Spanish came to Mexico in 1521, they brought milk, cheese, garlic, herbs and spices. Today, Mexican food includes recipes from all over the world, from the Caribbean to Africa.

MEXICO

Rosemary Hankin

Published in Great Britain in 2018 by Wayland

Produced for Wayland by Calcium

Dewey Number: 641.3'00972-dc23
ISBN: 978 0 7502 9689 2

10 9 8 7 6 5 4 3 2 1

MIX
Paper from
responsible sources
FSC® C104740

Wayland
An imprint of
Hachette Children's Group
Part of Hodder & Stoughton
Carmelite House
50 Victoria Embankment
London EC4Y 0DZ

An Hachette UK Company
www.hachette.co.uk

www.hachettechildrens.co.uk

Printed in China

Picture Acknowledgements:
Dreamstime: Pablo Caridad 9t, Crispi 9b, Uli Danner 13b, Jerl71 13t, Jeffrey Kreulen 5tl, Lunamarina 4, 5tr, Per Olsson 5b, Arturo Osorno 21t, Pipa100 7l, Jaime Leonardo Gonzalez Salazar 17b, Yurchyk 7r; Shutterstock: Azucar 25t, Bonchan 18, Joe Gough 10, Holbox 21b, Katie Smith Photography 25b, Nayashkova Olga 14, Ruth Peterkin 17t, Lori Sparkia 22, Nathalie Speliers Ufermann 26, Wavebreakmedia 6. Tudor Photography: 11, 15, 19, 23, 27.

Some parts of Mexico have amazing rock formations.

Mexicans love to party! Their festivals are full of bright, fun, colourful decorations, such as these piñatas.

Hot and flavoursome chillies are used in many Mexican dishes.

Get Ready to Cook

Cooking is fun! There's nothing better than making food to share with your family and friends.

Every recipe page in this book starts with a 'You will need' list. This is a set of ingredients. Make sure you collect everything on the list before you start cooking.

Look out for the 'Top tips' boxes. These have great tips to help you cook.

'Be safe!' boxes warn you when you need to be extra careful.

Use one chopping board for meat and fish and a different chopping board for vegetables and fruit.

Always ask a grown-up if you can do some cooking.

Watch out for sharp knives! Ask a grown-up to help you with chopping and cutting.

Make sure you wash your hands before you start cooking.

Always wash any fruit and vegetables before using them.

Always ask a grown-up for help when cooking on the hob or using the oven.

Wear an apron to keep your clothes clean as you cook.

Southern Surprises

Southern Mexicans love chicken dishes such as kebabs, rice dishes, stews and soups. They cook with lots of onion and garlic. Also on the menu are tangy vegetables, flavoured with chilli and spices such as cinnamon, oregano and coriander. Mexicans eat these dishes as a main course or as a side dish.

Everyday meals

Tortillas are loved by Mexican people and are eaten almost every day. In the state of Oaxaca they are served with a special sauce called mole, which is made from different ingredients including bananas and peanut butter. Rich chocolate drinks are often served in Oaxaca, and the Mexicans here love cocoa so much they use it in savoury dishes!

Insect delights

Grasshoppers live only in some states of Mexico, including Oaxaca, and here they are eaten! *Chapulines* are grasshoppers fried with garlic, chilli and onions until they are crisp. They are served with lime juice.

Southern Mexico is full of wonders, including the Mayan ruins at Tulum.

Chapulines are eaten as a crispy snack or a tasty *taco* filling.

9

Chicken Enchiladas

You will need:

olive oil
2 skinless, boneless chicken
  breast fillets, cubed
½ onion, chopped
100 g sour cream
100 g Cheddar cheese, grated
1 tsp dried parsley
pinch of dried oregano
pinch of ground black pepper
100 g plain tomato sauce
4 tbsp water
1 tsp chilli powder
1 garlic clove, crushed
3 soft tortillas
50 g prepared
  enchilada sauce
fresh parsley,
  chopped

Wrapping food in soft corn tortillas dates back thousands of years to Mayan times. Garlic, chilli and oregano are popular flavourings that are used in a lot of Mexican food, including this delicious dish.

BE SAFE!
• Ask a grown-up to help you chop the chicken and onion.
• Be careful when you sauté on the hob.

Step 1

Preheat the oven to 180°C. In a non-stick pan, sauté the chicken in olive oil until the meat is no longer pink and the juices run clear.

Step 2

Stir in the chopped onion, sour cream, just over half the cheese, the parsley, oregano and pepper. Heat through until the cheese melts. Stir in the tomato sauce, water, chilli powder and crushed garlic.

Step 3

Spoon equal amounts of the chicken mixture on to each tortilla. Roll them up carefully and arrange in a baking dish. Spoon the enchilada sauce across the top. Scatter the remaining cheese on top.

Step 4

Place the dish in the oven and bake uncovered for 20 minutes. Cool for 10 minutes before serving, then garnish with fresh, chopped parsley.

TOP TIP Why not add some chopped green pepper in step 2? Tasty!

The Valley of Mexico

The Valley of Mexico is in central Mexico. In 1821, Mexico became independent of Spain. To celebrate, the Mexicans in the city of Puebla, in the Valley of Mexico, held a huge feast. The nuns of the city made a delicious new dish for the feast, which used all the colours of the Mexican flag, green, white and red. The delicious dish is called *chile en nogada*.

Sweet and spicy

To make chile en nogada, large poblano peppers are stuffed with lots of cooked meats and dried fruit such as raisins and dates. The peppers are then fried. Next, a creamy walnut sauce is poured over the peppers and they are decorated with pomegranate seeds.

Big and bustling

Central Mexico is the busiest and most modern part of the country. In the capital, Mexico City, Mexicans love to eat meat such as beef, pork, goat, lamb and mutton. *Birria* is a slow-cooked dish of goat or mutton with dried, roasted peppers. It is served with soup and tacos. Sausages are popular in central Mexico, especially chorizos. These spicy sausages are served fresh or smoked with chillies.

Many Mexican buildings are painted in pretty, bright colours. This is the city of Guanajuato in central Mexico.

Mexicans love to eat sausages in all shapes and sizes! They are made in long strings and sold in local markets.

13

Chilli Beef Tortillas

You will need:

olive oil
1 onion, chopped
1 garlic clove, crushed
450 g minced beef
400 g tin chopped tomatoes
400 g tin kidney beans, drained
200 g tin sweetcorn
1 red pepper, seeded
   and chopped
1 tsp chilli powder
1 tsp paprika
salt, to taste
120 ml water
12 soft tortillas
Cheddar cheese,
   grated
fresh parsley

Chilli beef is a great Mexican dish. It used to be made with chopped beef, but is now usually made with minced beef. There are many recipes for chilli beef. This one is spicy, but not too hot!

BE SAFE!
• Ask a grown-up to help you chop the vegetables.
• Always wear oven gloves when using the oven.

Step 1

Heat some olive oil in a large pan. Then fry the onion and garlic, stirring until soft. Add the minced beef and cook until browned. Stir occasionally.

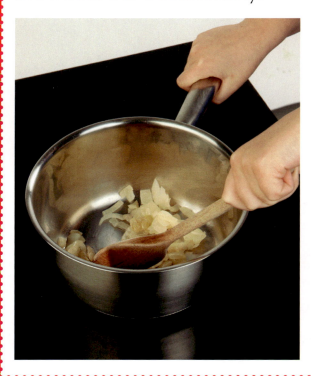

Step 2

Add the other ingredients, excluding the tortillas, cheese and parsley. Put the lid on the pan, turn down the heat, and simmer the chilli beef for 30 minutes. Stir every now and then to stop the beef from sticking to the pan. Preheat the oven to 180˚C.

Step 3

Place the tortillas in a stack and wrap them in foil. This will stop them from drying out. Place them in the oven and cook for 15 minutes.

Step 4

Wearing oven gloves, take the tortillas out of the oven and remove the foil. Fill the tortillas with the chilli beef and grated cheese, then wrap them. Garnish with parsley.

TOP TIP To make your chilli beef extra-spicy, add 1 tsp cayenne pepper and a bit more chilli powder!

Near the Border

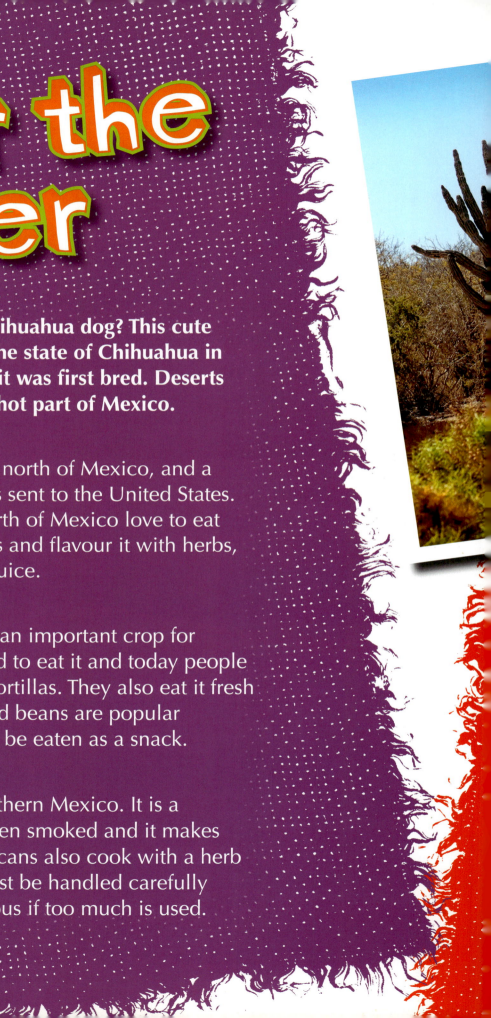

Have you heard of a Chihuahua dog? This cute little dog is named after the state of Chihuahua in Northern Mexico, where it was first bred. Deserts are found in this dry and hot part of Mexico.

Beef lovers

Cattle are farmed in the north of Mexico, and a lot of beef from the area is sent to the United States. People who live in the north of Mexico love to eat beef. They cook thin slices and flavour it with herbs, spices, garlic and lemon juice.

Maize on the menu

Maize, or sweetcorn, is an important crop for Mexicans. The Aztecs used to eat it and today people use it to make tacos and tortillas. They also eat it fresh as corn on the cob. Refried beans are popular as a side dish, or they can be eaten as a snack.

Smoke and spices

Chipotle is made in northern Mexico. It is a jalapeño chilli that has been smoked and it makes dishes hot, hot, hot! Mexicans also cook with a herb called *epazote*, which must be handled carefully because it can be poisonous if too much is used.

Cactus plants grow in the Mexican desert near to the United States border.

Sweetcorn is used for many delicious dishes and also for fun decorations. Corn kernels are dyed bright colours and sold in outdoor markets in northern Mexico.

Guacamole

You will need:

4 mild chillies, chopped
2 fresh tomatoes, chopped
1 white onion, chopped
pinch of salt
juice of ½ lime
3 ripe avocados
fresh parsley

The Aztecs first made tasty guacamole hundreds of years ago. When the Spanish came to Mexico, they loved the dish and it is now popular all over the world!

BE SAFE!
• Never rub your eyes when handling chillies. They will really sting!
• Ask a grown-up to prepare the avocados.

Step 1

Place the chillies, tomatoes, onion and salt in a food processor. Blend until the mixture forms a smooth paste. Add the lime juice and blend again to mix.

Step 2

Using a sharp knife, cut the avocados in half lengthways. Then separate the two halves. Remove the stone and scoop out the flesh using a spoon. Place in a mixing bowl.

Step 3

Mash the avocado flesh with a fork. Don't mash it for too long. You need to leave a few lumps for some texture. Add the tomato mixture and stir into the avocado until mixed.

TOP TIP If the mixture in the food processor is too stiff, add some water.

Step 4

Transfer the guacamole to a serving dish and garnish with fresh parsley leaves. Serve with some tortilla chips or crisps.

Pacific Side

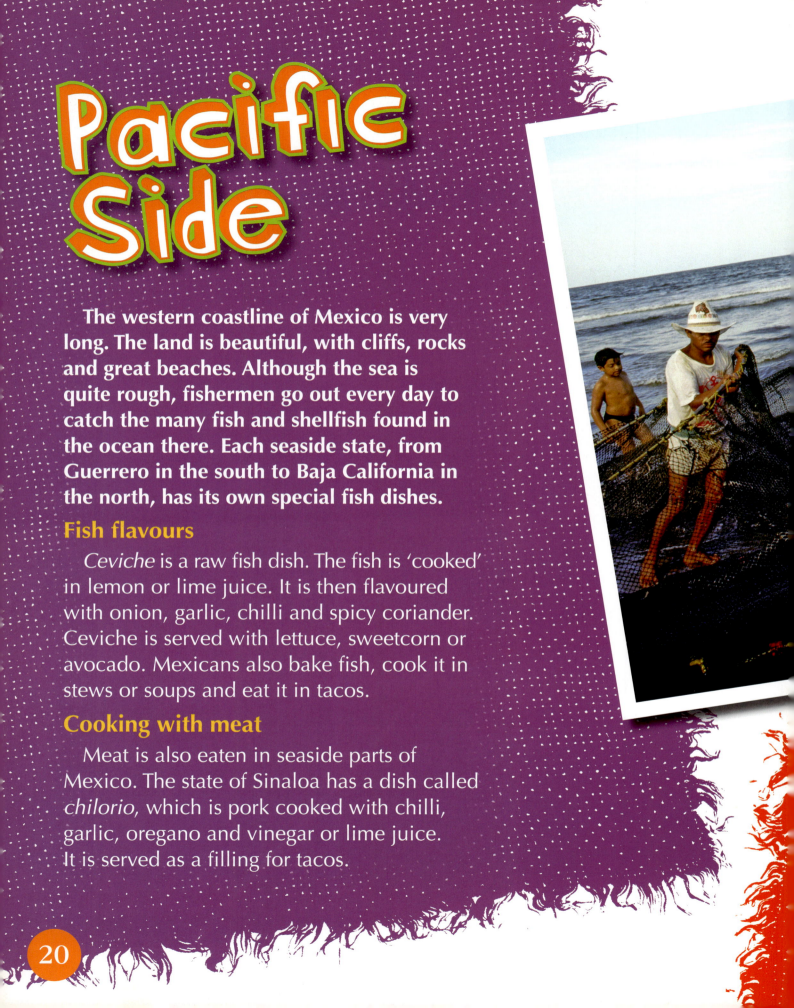

The western coastline of Mexico is very long. The land is beautiful, with cliffs, rocks and great beaches. Although the sea is quite rough, fishermen go out every day to catch the many fish and shellfish found in the ocean there. Each seaside state, from Guerrero in the south to Baja California in the north, has its own special fish dishes.

Fish flavours

Ceviche is a raw fish dish. The fish is 'cooked' in lemon or lime juice. It is then flavoured with onion, garlic, chilli and spicy coriander. Ceviche is served with lettuce, sweetcorn or avocado. Mexicans also bake fish, cook it in stews or soups and eat it in tacos.

Cooking with meat

Meat is also eaten in seaside parts of Mexico. The state of Sinaloa has a dish called *chilorio*, which is pork cooked with chilli, garlic, oregano and vinegar or lime juice. It is served as a filling for tacos.

In Mexico, some people fish from the shore using huge nets. These fishermen have made a good catch!

Prawns have been added to this ceviche. The dish has lots of sharp, tangy flavours.

21

Tomato Salsa

The Spanish word 'salsa' means 'sauce'. You could try this delicious mixture with Chilli Beef Tortillas, on pages 14 and 15. Salsa can be eaten cooked or uncooked. Either way, it has quite a kick!

You will need:

2 tbsp corn oil, plus extra for brushing
2 fresh chillies
1 small red onion, chopped
4 garlic cloves, peeled
6 fresh tomatoes, halved and seeded
salt and ground black pepper
juice of 2 limes
4 tbsp fresh coriander, chopped

BE SAFE!
- Be careful when you fry and use the hob.
- Ask a grown-up to grill the tomatoes for you.

Step 1

Put the grill on high. Heat the corn oil in a small pan and then fry the chillies, red onion and garlic until the mixture is soft.

Step 2

Brush the tomatoes with corn oil. Season well with salt and ground black pepper. Grill the tomatoes on both sides until slightly charred and soft.

Step 3

Place the tomatoes and the chilli mixture in a food processor. Add the lime juice and blend until the mixture is smooth. Add the chopped coriander and blend briefly again, or pulse a few times.

Step 4

Taste some of the salsa. You can add more salt and ground black pepper, if you wish. Then spoon the tomato salsa into a serving dish. Serve your salsa as a delicious dip with crisps or tortilla chips.

TOP TIP For fresh, uncooked salsa, finely chop the vegetables. Mix them with the lime juice, coriander and seasoning.

Ancient Ways

The Yucatán Peninsula is at the south-eastern tip of Mexico. It is near the Caribbean, and some of the cooking methods used here come from Jamaica and other nearby countries.

Mighty Mayans

The Yucatán Peninsula is where the Mayans built their great cities. Many Mayan foods are still eaten here today, such as *chaya*. This is a green leaf vegetable that must be cooked before it is safe to eat. The Mayans also used achiote, a spice made from the seeds of the annatto tree. Achiote gives food flavour and turns it a rich, golden colour.

Meaty meals

The Yucatán people cook turkey and venison. They also like pork, which they sometimes wrap in banana leaves and roast in an underground oven.

Sweet surprises

Sweet treats are made everywhere in Mexico. Mexicans love fritters served with syrup or honey, fruit-filled doughnuts and biscuits. They also eat candied nuts and even candied cactus! Sweet dishes are often made for religious festivals.

'Day of the Dead' sugar skulls are made in Mexico to celebrate the lives of people who have died.

The seeds of the annatto tree are taken out of their prickly cases, dried and used whole or ground in Mexican dishes.

Day of the Dead Bread

You will need:

750 g plain flour
100 g caster sugar
1 tsp salt
1 tbsp anise seed
2 packets dried yeast
120 ml milk
120 ml water
110 g butter
4 eggs
icing sugar, for
    sprinkling
2 tbsp orange
    juice

'Day of the Dead' is a festival day during which Mexicans believe they are visited by the spirits of their dead relatives. Delicious food is eaten, such as this sugared bread which is decorated with bones!

BE SAFE!

- Ask a grown-up for help with this recipe.
- Be careful when you are using the hob and oven.

Step 1

Mix 190 g of flour, the sugar, salt, anise and yeast in a large bowl. Heat the milk, water and butter in a pan.

Step 2

Beat the milk mixture into the flour mixture. Add the eggs and mix well. Slowly add the rest of the flour.

Step 3

Knead the mixture on a floured surface for 10 minutes. Place in a greased bowl and leave to rise until doubled in size.

Step 4

Shape the dough into loaves. Make 'bones' from some of the dough and use it to decorate the loaves. Place them on a baking tray and leave to rise for 1 hour. Preheat the oven to 180°C.

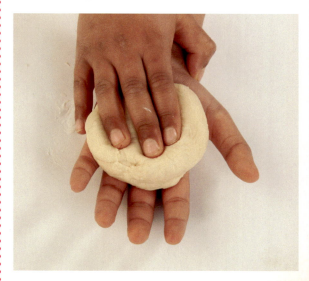

Step 5

Bake your loaves for around 20-30 minutes. After baking, brush some orange juice over the loaves and sprinkle them with the sugar. Leave to cool.

TOP TIP Why not sprinkle your loaves with coloured sugar for a pretty finish?

Mexican Meals on the Map!

Chihuahua

Gulf of California

Baja California

Tomato salsa

Chilli beef tortillas

Now that you have discovered how to cook the delicious foods of Mexico, find out where they are cooked and eaten on this map of the country.

Guacamole

United States

Day of the
Dead bread

Gulf of
Mexico

Mexico

The Yucatán Peninsula

Caribbean Sea

MEXICO CITY

Guerrero   Oaxaca

PACIFIC OCEAN

Chicken
enchiladas

29

Glossary

Aztecs People who created a great empire in Mexico hundreds of years ago.

charred Slightly blackened from heat.

cocoa A powder that is made from cocoa pods and used to flavour food.

desert An area that has almost no rain and so has very few plants.

enchilada A soft corn tortilla wrapped around a mix of savoury ingredients and covered with sauce.

festival A large celebration in which many people take part.

garnish To decorate food before serving.

ingredients Different foods and seasonings that are used to make a recipe.

kebab A meal of roasted meat cooked on a skewer and eaten with bread.

Mayans People who lived in the Yucatán area thousands of years ago.

nuns Women who take a vow to spend their lives in the service of God.

sauté To lightly fry food in oil or butter.

savoury Food that is not sweet in taste.

seasoning Salt, pepper and other herbs and spices that give food certain flavours.

spices Powders that are rich in taste and are used to add flavour to food.

tacos A fried tortilla folded around ingredients such as meat and cheese.

tropical forests Forests with a very high rainfall.

volcanoes Openings in the Earth's crust from which lava flows.

Further Reading

Mexico (A True Book), Elaine Landau, Scholastic

Mexico (Destination Detectives), Jen Green, Raintree

Mexico (Unpacked), Susie Brooks, Wayland

Websites

This is a great site for information on all aspects of life in Mexico:
www.visitmexico.com

Check out the useful guides to Mexico's cities and states at this site:
www.mexonline.com/states.htm

This site has a lot of information about Mexican culture:
www.donquijote.org/culture/mexico/

Discover more about the varied arts of Mexico at the site of this museum dedicated to the subject:
www.nationalmuseumofmexicanart.org

Index